FLAT TAX ON WEALTH

AND HOW IT CAN SAVE OUR COUNTRY

PETER BUTTERFIELD

All world rights reserved.

Copyright© 2014 by Peter Butterfield.

No part of this book may be reproduced or distributed in any form or by any means or stored in a database or retrieval system, except as permitted under Sections 107 or 108 of the U.S. Copyright Act without prior written permission of the publisher or author.

This book and all information contained therein, is the opinion of the author and meant for informational and educational purposes only. The ideas, views, and suggestions contained in this book, including those that relate to the United States federal tax system, are that of the author and do not necessarily reflect those shared by the publisher or others mentioned in this book. Any third party references are for informational purposes only and the author has not necessarily endorsed, approved, or affiliated with any such third party. The author makes no representations or warranties regarding the accuracy of the information, none of which is meant to be financial, accounting, investment, tax, trading, or legal advice. Neither the author nor the publisher is engaged in rendering professional advice or services to the individual readers. Any reader should independently verify the accuracy of any information in this book and seek his or her own professional advice and representation from a licensed professional before making any decision.

Neither the publisher nor author assumes any liability for any errors or omissions, or for how this book or its contents are used or interpreted, or for any consequences resulting directly or indirectly from use of this book. The author shall not be liable or responsible for any loss, injury, or damage to a reader or any third party for any decision made or action based upon reliance on or use of the information in this book.

I dedicate this book to the Aldrich brothers
Bob
Bill
Nate
John
and to those who served with them.

Contents

Foreword 7

Introduction 9

Chapter 1 Ideal Tax System 11

   National Debt Graph 14

Chapter 2 Its the Pits 15

Chapter 3 Flat Tax on Wealth and its Advantages 21

Chapter 4 Difficulties 29

Chapter 5 Social Engineering 35

Chapter 6 Best Tax 41

Chapter 7 Other Wealth Tax systems 53

Chapter 8 Interrelated Tax Matters 55

Acknowledgments 59

Foreword

When I was a kid, Dad said, "You can have any thing you want—anything in the world—as long as you can pay for it."

"Want a pair of roller skates? No problem! How about a scooter?" (He built me one, as did most dads of our era, out of a couple of boards and the wheels from an old pair of roller skates.) "A bicycle?" (On the way back from the Jersey Shore when I was six, he bought me a bicycle a man was offering on his front porch for $9, dickering the seller down, first to $7, then to $5.) "Car? Boat? Airplane? It's yours, as long as you can pay for it."

Of course, the corollary was his real message:

If you can't pay for it, you can't have it.

In later years that wisdom was supplemented with:

Get out of debt.
Stay out of debt.

Later on, I myself added one more caveat: don't borrow to bet!

Those timeless words form the premise of this book.

Introduction

"But in this world nothing can be said to be certain, except death and taxes."
Benjamin Franklin — 13 Nov 1789
Letter to Jean Baptiste Le Roy

Others might concern themselves with how to delay death, but my focus in life has been taxes. Specifically, I have spent months of study on how to fix our country's tax structure, which I consider nothing short of a catastrophe.

In this book, I will make a case for the elimination of personal federal income taxes, an unwieldy tax that is complex, unfair, and insufficient to stem the red tide of our country's deficit spending. I would also argue to eliminate taxes on corporations and businesses, the engines of our economy.

My proposal is to replace the progressive income tax with a flat tax on an individual's total wealth, no matter if an individual is poor, middle class, or rich. This new approach would mean we could, at last, dispense with the hundreds of exemptions and rules that make up the 74,000-page U.S. Income Tax Code—a tax system so onerous and complicated that 8 out of 10 Americans must seek assistance in filling out their tax forms.

And how much time does it take? All told, U.S. taxpayers and businesses spend about *7.6 billion hours a year* complying with the filing requirements of the Internal Revenue Code. [1]

My approach would result in a tax system that not only provides transparency and equity, but would also require a contribution to our country's operational costs that is truly based on ability to pay. This book is a clarion call to all those who have wondered, with alarm, how to fix what ails this country.

Chapter 1

An Ideal Tax System

We all hate taxes. One obvious way to lower them is to get rid of wasteful and unnecessary government spending. Still, when all is said and done, taxes must be collected somehow in order to pay for whatever government we have in a free market system.

Some amount of tax revenue is essential for national defense, infrastructure, courts, titles, the reliable registration of legal agreements, property surveys, law enforcement, and prisons—all elements of a modern democracy that operate on the premise of private property rights. How would those rights be proven without a proper court system or deed registry? What would life be like without roads, bridges, tunnels, transit systems (whether publicly or privately owned or built), schools, and airports?

Even in a non-free market economy, the equivalent of a tax must still be present in some way, imposed by whatever regime reigns. But taxes should be straightforward and fair, not hidden or buried to compensate those in power. Not disproportionately paid by those who don't possess the means to get around indecipherable tax laws.

My focus then is to zero in on the U.S. tax system and propose a new approach that taxes wealth, not income.

Let us first consider the five key elements of an "Ideal Tax System" and consider their limitations.

1. Affordable

2. Fair

3. Not overly complicated

4. Socially engineered

       a) Income/wealth leveling

       b) Limited tax breaks for special causes

5. Encourages wealth building

Now let's test our current tax system to see how well it meets these requirements.

1. AFFORDABLE

Clearly we have not covered the cost of the country's expenditures with our present tax code. (While this manuscript concerns itself with the U.S. Income Tax Code, much the same criticism applies to many state tax systems as well.) As of February 25, 2014, the official debt of the United States government stood at $17.4 trillion —an equivalent of $142,245 per household, according to justfacts.com, the website for Just Facts, a non-profit research and educational institute. (See graph on page 16.)

2. FAIR

Federal income tax rates would have had to more than *double* across all incomes if Congress were to pay up the deficit in fiscal year 2010, according to an article on a 2010 report issued by the nonpartisan Tax Foundation.

Instead of taxing joint filers with rates ranging from 10 percent to 35 percent, tax rates would have to start at 24.3 percent and reach a whopping 84.9 percent, according to the TaxFoundation.org article.

"The federal government is spending so much that even if policymakers were willing to fund government services with actual tax revenue instead of piling on more debt, the federal income tax system in its current form wouldn't be able to raise that much," said Tax Foundation Director of Policy and Communications Bill Ahern in the article.

Ahern also said that if no changes were made in the tax code or spending patterns, the income tax system couldn't raise as much revenue as the government plans to spend for the foreseeable future. [2]

Tax rates of the very rich—including federal, state and local—would come close to 100 percent with the requisite 8 percent increase, the article stated.

"At some point, government would be taking away all earnings and there would be no incentive to work," Ahern said. "There can be little doubt that the high tax rates necessary to balance the budget in the next several years would discourage all income-producing endeavors."

Is that "fair"? I certainly think not. I believe it grossly unfair.

3. NOT OVERLY COMPLICATED

The present federal tax code is impossibly complex. It has grown, page after page, over the past 75 years or so, into a wedding cake of special tax breaks, penalties, requirements, and particular circumstances benefiting or penalizing this or that taxpayer. At the horrendous size of nearly 74,000 pages, it surely fails the test of being "not overly complicated."

4. SOCIALLY ENGINEERED

The progressive tax and our tax code, in general, is designed to even out some of the more obvious and extreme disparities in income between the rich and the poor and to provide for socially desirable causes such as retirement income, education, health care, and a safety net for the poor. But even with these best of "social engineering" intentions, it *still* fails to consistently tax individuals of great wealth!

5. ENCOURAGES WEALTH BUILDING

Finally, how can we best resolve the seeming contradictions between legitimate goals of social engineering and wealth building? Can we, and more importantly, *should we*, try to avoid the concentrations of great wealth in few hands? We will touch on some of this in later chapters.

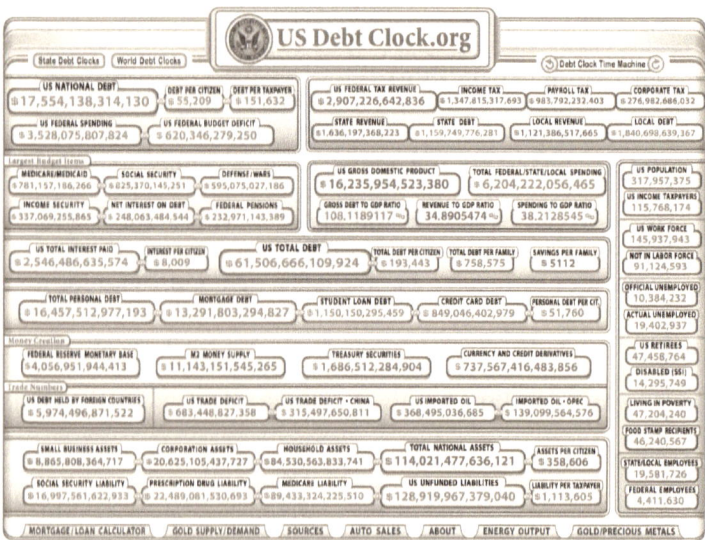

A screenshot from 4-10-14.

Chapter 2

It's the PITs!

IT'S THE PERSONAL INCOME TAX

Clearly, our government has a problem with decades of unsustainable spending. But our resulting deficits were also created by the failure of the Personal Income Tax. The tax code calls it "Your Federal Income Tax—For Individuals." The simplified version of the present tax code is wrong-headed for various reasons.

1. The IRS has been sent out to chase a chimera, a fleeting glimpse of wealth or wealth *in transit*. It doesn't tax wealth where it is and likely will be for a long time.

2. Why would any wise government take income gain from an individual? That gain has the potential to create or increase wealth! Why would a wise tax collector give a refund, a rebate, or a tax credit because of money lost in one

year? The taxpayer could still have prodigious wealth and pay nothing.

3. The PIT is simply a convenient red herring to lure politicians (or more correctly, serve as a foil for the politicians) to rant and rave and cook up special tax avoidance clauses be put into law by those same politicians. In recent years, the federal government has printed and distributed *Publication 17, Your Federal Income Tax for Individuals*, a book of around 300 pages, available free to every taxpayer (and paid for by the same taxpayers, who are buried by taxes). *Publication 17* covers the essence of the federal PIT, but the full PIT occupied 4,333 pages of the Federal tax code in 2008. [3]

WHO SAYS WHAT?

My small voice is nearly drowned out by the crescendo, the absolute cacophony of competing voices on the radio, on TV, in carefully authored newspaper and magazine articles, and in entire books that complain about our tax system.

U.S. Rep. John Boehner thinks we should not raise taxes on anyone, rich or poor. [4] President Barack Obama says we should increase taxes on only those making more $250,000 per married couple in a household. [5] U.S. Sen. Chuck Schumer says he thinks the lower limit should be set at $1 million. The recently created bi-partisan commission says we are headed for a catastrophe if we do not get rid of the special entitlements. [6] An email in circulation compares our income tax with European income and value-added tax rates, which is defined as the sale price charged to the customer minus the cost of materials and other taxable inputs. [7] Writer Froma Harrop tears into John Kerry for the enormous income his household enjoys from leasing his private Gulfstream jet and the Heinz family fortune. [8] Others subdivide the "rich" into the "lower upper class" and the "ultra-rich."

Walter Williams has pointed out that, according to the Tax Policy Center, nearly half of U.S. households pay no federal income taxes, either because their incomes are too low or because their higher incomes are offset by credits, deductions, and exemptions! [9]

Despite the deeply conflicting views, no one disagrees with Nina Olson, the country's official national taxpayer advocate. (Her position was created in 2006 by Congress, which has ignored her ever since.) She argues that the tax code's complexity is one of the most serious problems facing taxpayers. The federal tax code, 400 pages long in 1913, has swollen to more than 70,000 pages. Olson wrote that "An incredible 82 percent of taxpayers are so flummoxed that they pay for help." Sixty percent hire an accountant and another 22 percent use tax software. Olson referred to one year's update of the tax code as the CPA's guaranteed income and retirement plan. [10]

Let me be clear: my proposal is a radical change to the present system, but would not totally eliminate the complexity of our tax system. It would greatly simplify the system by focusing on a valid basis for our federal income taxes.

We can argue about where the money should go, who should get the benefit, and how much should be spent. My principal concern in this document is, *Where should the money come from*?

ORIGINAL SIN

Let me pause for a moment and touch on a different, but important question: how did this taxing catastrophe come about?

The short answer is social engineering. Efforts during the last century to indulge in social engineering by granting special tax breaks for one class or another have resulted in a complete hodgepodge of tax law. The law is not only complex, but often achieves contradictory or conflicting results to those it intended to help. Much of this is addressed in Chapter 5, "On Social Engineering."

SHOW ME THE MONEY

So again: *Where do we find sufficient revenue?* Today's Personal Income Tax is the wrong answer: It is, quite literally, the pits! And I believe it CANNOT come from the lower or middle class! There isn't enough money even if much of their income was taken.

It necessarily must come from the wealthy. As Willy Sutton said, "That's where the money is!"

The real solution is a Flat Tax on Wealth (FTOW).

In our large, mature country, economists predict a natural average growth rate of wealth at around 1.5 percent per year, although differences in the rate may result from:

a) Changes in population

b) Development in new technology

c) Foreign entities acquiring or divesting assets in the U.S.

d) Acquisition of foreign assets

e) Calamity, natural or man-made

Chapter 3

A Flat Tax on Wealth and its Advantages

A FLAT TAX ON WEALTH IS NOT A NEW CONCEPT.

One of the more ardent and capable supporters of a tax on wealth is Edward Wolff, who documented the inordinately high disparity between the very rich and the rest of us here in the United States. He pointed out that the U.S. is "much more unequal than any other advanced industrial country." One outcome of the tremendous disparity in the U.S. is that the bottom 20 percent has "basically zero wealth." [11]

The important difference between Wolff's plan and my own is simply that his proposal is really a kind of surtax, exempting the first $250,000 of wealth (80 percent of families would pay nothing) and then increasing progressively from 2 percent to 8 percent for those with wealth of $5 million and greater. That $250,000 figure certainly looks like an Obama benchmark to me.

In their book, *Reckless Endangerment*, Gretchen Morgenson and Joshua Rosner wrote that in 1996, "A key plank of presidential candidate Steve Forbes platform, a flat tax would have eliminated all individual deductions in exchange for lowering the overall tax rate from the mid-30s to 19 percent." But their proposal is for a flat tax on income, not wealth.

In another interesting and relevant paper, "Taxing Wealth—What For?"author Jan Schnellenbach cites classical normative principles of taxation. On the one hand, he prefers not to replace income taxes but to superimpose a wealth tax on top of those taxes for the super rich. On the other hand, he seems to argue that the mal-distribution of capital simply leads to even greater incomes. But that's acceptable, he contends, because these high incomes are already properly taxed (or are taxable at a higher rate, if needed) because of the many built-in protections that take effect when warranted. Thus, changing from a tax on income to a tax on wealth is a pointless exercise.

2 PERCENT

I suggest using a 2 percent tax on net wealth (assets minus liabilities) as a starting point for discussion, but not arbitrarily so.

2005 is the latest year that provides tax figures for coincident personal income and wealth from published U. S. government data. [12] Polina Vlasenko, a senior research fellow for the American Institute of Economic Research, asserted that the total wealth of U.S. households in 2005 was about $58.1 trillion. Federal data also reflected that the adjusted gross income was about $7.5 trillion and the total income tax paid by those households was $935 billion.[13]

A 1.75 percent tax on wealth would be sufficient to replace, in its entirety, the revenue from the Personal Income Tax. But it would not be sufficient to pay for annual federal expenditures which would have required a roughly 2.3percent tax on wealth to achieve a "balanced budget" (assuming the expenditures at that time). But even a 2.3 percent rate will not be sufficient as future Social Security, Medicare and Medicaid expenses projected for the years ahead come due.

However, I'm using the 2 percent as a starting point for discussion purposes because, in the end, if you can't pay for it, you can't have it. And I truly believe that we will need, as a nation, to cut back on expenditures and that should reduce the need for higher taxes."

Here are some of the advantages of FTOW under my proposed plan:

1. Tax simplification is the obvious, immediate benefit. Bank and brokerage statements provide accessible and accurate accounting for the vast proportion of major liquid assets. The county assessor's office provides assessed values for homes and other kinds of real estate.

2. The tax rate remains fixed. It is neither progressive nor regressive, but inherently neutral. All pay at the same rate, with no tailored rate for the wealthy or poor. If a person is worth $50 billion, he pays $1 billion at a tax rate of 2 percent. If another is worth $50,000, he pays $1,000 in tax at the same 2 percent rate.

3. It eliminates the need for special "long-term" or "short-term" treatment of capital gains, a major advantage to the 180 million of us who are plagued by this preposterous, burdensome tax that requires extraordinary record keeping. The mandated accounting inhibits our freely buying and

selling of stocks since our present attention is focused on keeping an investment one year or longer to avoid punitive tax rates, a senseless element of our present personal income tax system.

5. A tax on wealth tax eliminates the need for an alternative minimum tax (AMT) altogether. Since the FTOW inherently takes more from those with greater wealth, a special tax to hit the wealthy becomes redundant and unnecessary.

6. The tax on wealth is superior in concept to the value-added tax (VAT). Although Steve Forbes and others have pushed for a valued added tax, a consumption tax that's common in Europe, it carries three disadvantages when compared to a flat tax on wealth:

a) There is an inherent unfairness in such a tax on discretionary spending. If one of our wealthier citizens spends $2 million in a year, his consumption tax of $500,000 will reduce his total wealth of $5 billion by a mere .1 percent. But if John Doe is levied the same consumption tax of $500,000 from his (mere) $10 million, he will have decreased his remaining wealth by a full 5 percent. That's

50 times the percentage loss, leaving him with only $9.5 million of his remaining wealth.

b) Most similar proposals suggest that those with less than a certain specified limit should pay no tax on the first $10,000 spent (or some other amount, depending on the politician involved) in order to reduce the impact on the poor. But a flat wealth tax, once established, would eliminate the probable, constant political haggling over taxes involved. Our Congress could then focus on the overall budget and the ultimate level of FTOW taxation required without getting into who should pay for it.

c) Forbes has claimed that with a value-added tax, we could get rid of the IRS [14]. This is preposterous. Some governmental entity must exist with the responsibility to collect and disperse the tax revenue. Even though corporations and wealthy individuals would principally be involved, they can afford even more clever accountants and lawyers to find ways to get around such a tax. Surely careful auditing is required, no matter the tax scheme. But, once again, tracking the spending of individuals would require a burdensome bureaucracy, the very thing the VAT is supposed to eliminate.

7. Forbes, in 1996 and again in 2000, based his entire presidential campaign on a 17 percent flat tax. While this has some of the advantages of a true tax on wealth (it would be neither "progressive" nor "regressive"), it simply ignores the underlying difficulties presented in discretionary spending and raising sufficient revenue from the lower and middle-income families who spend less.

8. The wealth of foreigners would be taxed at the same rate as U.S. citizens. This may be a drawback in that some foreigners might prefer to withdraw from U.S. markets. But they would then forfeit the advantages of our markets. So they would be free to choose.

9. Under normal circumstances, wealth is less variable than income. So the tax yield is less variable, making planning easier for the individual taxed, the tax authorities and those who plan for the use of the money. (As a note, the recession year of 2008 was not normal.)

10. Inflation and deflation are self-regulatory. If the economy inflates, taxes go up accordingly. When the economy drops, wealth and tax revenues drop. When a politician decides we "ABSOLUTELY MUST HAVE" additional funds for some grave emergency, the citizenry can be rightly alarmed. Clearly such a cry would signal that the nation is being called upon for some undertaking beyond its means! It had better be a true crisis, i.e., that if the funding isn't forthcoming, it will be the end of the United States as we know it.

11. Because wealth fluctuates over business cycles, a wise government would be prudent to build in a system of reserves when prosperity reigns to provide for times when the economy turns down. While Keynes argued for this, it is rarely accomplished. The smaller percentage fluctuation in wealth than in income should make budgeting for such eventualities smoother and easier. [15]

12. Because it is the objective of this study to move the tax base from "corporate earnings" to individual wealth, it is difficult for me to even think about suggesting adding other taxes to help cover the nation's expenses. In my judgment, any additional taxes should be used for the express purpose

of deterring unwanted or onerous behaviors, such as smoking, alcohol, or other drug use. The tax revenues could then be used to lessen the burden of a tax on wealth.

13. Revenues from other taxes—on oil, natural gas, or carbon, for example—can be factored in to reduce the tax on wealth to something less than 2 percent and ideally as little as 1 or 1.5 percent. Another example might be an approximate 1 percent federal tax on all sales and transfers of stocks and bonds that could be required by law. This will cut down on day trading and make it possible to track all such transactions much more easily. For the public at large, it should greatly reduce the volatility of stocks, bonds and mutual funds, and provide a far stronger sense of security for all investors. Violators would go to jail and pay heavy fines.

Chapter 4

Difficulties of a Flat Tax on Wealth

A flat tax on wealth would face plenty of difficulties. The devil is in the details. Should religious institutions be taxed or be given special tax treatment? Should ministers be taxed? Should entities with a negative net worth be given money? These are the easy questions.

More difficult issues include: How to measure wealth? When? What gets counted? An example of the trickier questions might be: What is an actor's film name worth in dollars? Does he own it, or does his studio? How about a writer's *nom-de-plume*?

Some of the answers can be suggested at the outset:

1. The U.S. Federal Reserve Bank or the U.S. Treasury must issue the only U.S. legal tender, as is the case today.

2. All U.S. banks must borrow *only* from a Federal Reserve Bank. The law would prohibit commercial bank-to-commercial bank and investment bank-to-investment bank

borrowing. This would immediately solve the "transparency" problem that was the principal and immediate cause of the recent liquidity crisis.

3. No "off-balance sheet" entries would be allowed by any entity—institution, partnership, or individual. Some reasonable dollar value would be required to be assigned to every entity on individual and corporate balance sheets and all necessary detail would be required to permit a reasonable audit and evaluation.

4. All cash transactions must be recorded. Cash must be considered taxable in the hands of the last entity to which it was credited.

5. I believe the measurement of the price of a stock (and thus its taxable worth) could be set as the year-end closing price or arranged as the "average" daily, weekly or monthly price of that stock during the trading year. There would have to be a special section to deal with catastrophic, year-end collapses in the market in such a way that normally the "average" value of assets would be taxed. However, in the event of such a collapse exceeding, say, 20 percent of the average, then either the year-end average or of the year-end

averages of the past five years might be used. This must then also apply in the event of a year-end upward burst in the value of investments.

6. Many non-real estate tangible assets are already taxed or licensed in some states (autos, boats, and airplanes), often by lower-level governmental entities. Their values (wealth) could be assigned using their figures. Another source could be insurance companies; if something is valuable enough, the owner would take the time and expense to insure it.

I don't really know how treasured antiques, especially family heirlooms are taxed today. But taxed they must be, if only as part of estate taxes. Art is likely to comprise only a small part of the wealth of most households, unless they are heavily traded. I venture to guess it would be a rare situation indeed in which an heir would have to sell an heirloom to afford the 1 percent or 2 percent annual tax on its value. It may be that antiques or family heirlooms would require some treatment clause in a FTOW, though I would prefer to minimize or eliminate all such special treatment. There are plenty of families today whose heirs have not lived up to the families' expectations and who have lost significant parts of a family estate. That is simply a household situation, which will neither be cured nor exacerbated by the tax on wealth; it is a fact of life.

There must be other accounting rules that would supplement these. Not being an accountant, I look to others for assistance with this suggestion.

7. One of the biggest challenges of a wealth tax? It's unconstitutional. The Constitution specifies that no federal "direct" tax may be collected unless it's divvied up between the states based on population. A state with twice the population, for example, would have to pay twice the wealth tax. A wealth tax is considered a "direct" tax because it is based on the value of a person's net assets at any given time.

Daniel Altman, a strong proponent of a wealth tax, believes a constitutional amendment could erase the requirement for geographic apportionment. He cites the Sixteenth Amendment, passed 18 years after the Supreme Court ruled that the income tax was a "direct" tax. The amendment authorized the government to impose an income tax without regard to the states' census numbers.

"The Sixteenth Amendment was ratified in 1913 so that the federal government could collect today's income tax. With public support, another amendment could certainly be added to allow a tax on wealth. It's been done before and can be done again," wrote Altman, a New York University economics instructor, in a Dec. 20, 2012, article on bigthink.com.

There is no question that numerous difficulties would need to be worked out. How should the federal government, for example, deal with valuable tangible assets such as works of art or various antiques? How do they become correctly valued or priced? How does one document existing debt? How does one put a value on federal retirement benefits or other annuities?

There are solutions to each of these challenges, such as applying the Black-Scholes model, a mathematical formula of the financial market that includes risk management and certain derivative investment instruments.

I believe that questions such as those regarding ministers and religious institutions and charities are present today. The change to a wealth tax makes these questions neither more difficult nor easier.

THE INCOME GAP

My proposed tax on wealth instead of income would go a long way toward solving a great many problems—monetarily, fiscally, socially, and, most importantly in my mind, ethically. Each challenge can and ought to be worked out, and it would likely take a lot less effort than what goes into the annual bickering over tax rates.

I genuinely believe that there is too great a difference between the wealth of individuals in our country. The rich grow richer, the poor grow *relatively* poorer. Yeah, I know, even the poor grow "richer" here and I have sometimes argued on that side of the issue.

One need only to look back in recent history to determine what's fueling this income gap. Thirty to 50 years ago, we used to get proxies for our stocks asking us to vote for a change in the corporate by-laws limiting the pay of officers and directors to no more than 20 times that of the average or sometimes the lowest paid employee. I believe that difference is now on the order of 400 times that average. To my mind, that is unnecessarily high, and we could well hire capable talent at the top for 1/10 that price.

But the problem is that the CEO "recommends" board members that then duly "vote" for higher salaries for the officers as being "necessary" to obtain the required high talent to advance the corporation. A clever caption under a *New Yorker* cartoon (a young woman talking to a guy at a cocktail party) reads: "True, a salary cap on Wall Street may limit the talent pool, but, on the other hand, if they get any more talented we'll all be broke."

To rein in these exorbitant salaries, I believe that legislation should require greater openness for shareholders as to the salaries and emoluments of executives and board members of corporations doing business in the United States, and permit shareholders, by law, to vote on them.

The income tax code is preposterously complex with deductions, exemptions, special considerations for this cause and that group, social, religious, military, retired, children, couples, elderly, dependents, making too much money, too little money, earning it here versus earning it overseas, tax losses in prior years versus the current year, how long one has owned a stock, treating interest versus earned income, whether income has been derived from social security or other income, and on and on and on.

My proposed tax on wealth would replace the personal income tax with a simple 2 percent annual tax on all wealth. I had originally hoped to keep the tax applicable only to those whose total wealth exceeded $20 million, but now believe that might not provide sufficient revenue to equal or exceed that generated by the present income tax which must be eliminated if my proposal is to succeed.

Chapter 5

On Social Engineering

The personal income tax has long been used as a vehicle for "social engineering," a concept that attempts to even out some of the more obvious and extreme disparities in income between the rich and the poor and to provide for socially desirable causes such as college education and home ownership. Although I would not deny the fact that it's been for the betterment of our society, I would make several arguments in favor of replacing the PIT with a flat tax on wealth.

Taxing a person's wealth in no way circumvents social engineering. It is simply a superior way of taxing true wealth instead of inferred wealth based on yearly income.

It's clear a very wealthy person ought to pay more in taxes than those in the average and lower-income brackets. The flat tax on wealth achieves exactly that.

GREAT ESTATES

Some well-known families (i.e., the Shrivers, Rockefellers, Kennedys, Fords, Waltons, Gates, Buffets, etc.) presumably have great personal wealth. But that wealth throws off far more income than they need—even to maintain mansions, luxurious gardens, additional homes, travel, yachts, club memberships, and aircraft.

As an example, let us assume that one has a wealth of $5 billion dollars or $5,000 million, as Rush Limbaugh likes to put it.

Let's make the further assumption that our subject has conservatively invested in funds, which net him 5 percent or $250 million annually after all expenses other than taxes. At a tax rate of 40 percent he would pay $100 million in federal personal income taxes. If we charge him 2 percent of his wealth, he would still pay the same $100 million

But if he could find a way to squeak by with an annual income of just $100 million dollars a year, his personal income tax would be reduced to $40 million, a $60 million reduction. In comparison, the flat tax on wealth would still collect the full $100 million.

In the first case, that $60 million savings to him and his family represents a net loss to the country as a whole and must be made up for by taxes paid by you and me. So here is a solid, superior social engineering benefit of the FTOW.

So the FTOW is "good" social engineering right at the outset.

FTOW AND CHARITABLE GIVING

It has been argued that the personal income tax encourages charitable giving. I disagree on two counts.

First, there is nothing particularly "charitable" about a gift made for tax reduction purposes. It is obviously just that—a gift made to reduce one's taxes and a deceptive practice.

Often, especially for really large bequests, a new foundation is created –and guess what—the person's son, daughter, cousin, girlfriend or neighbor is "elected" as the CEO or administrator.

With a flat tax on wealth, such a charitable gift deduction becomes unnecessary. Since the gift reduces the person's wealth by exactly the same amount as the gift, an individual's tax will be reduced by that same 1 percent or 2 percent—in effect, the very same amount.

TAX CREDITS

Tax credits are another tool often used to fund worthy causes. I think there is a better way. Let's say the goal is for all qualifying students to be provided funds for college. Then I would recommend passing legislation to give such a stipend from the U.S. Treasury rather than encourage it with a tax credit. Such programs could be amended or improved, such as including a stipend for trade schools, distance learning classes and on-line universities. I have no problem with that approach, but amending the tax code requires re-writing the tax publications, re-education of tax accountants and tax attorneys, in addition to financial advisors.

If we need to discourage some practice, such as the consumption of gasoline, oil, or imported oil only, then don't bother with tax credits. Tax it! In my opinion, there is no need to subsidize or legislate vehicle standards. Consumers themselves will buy the most efficient, least costly vehicles to drive.

What I deem the most valid criticism of all is when tax credits or taxpayer-funded, social programs are pushed too far in the pursuit of social engineering. It creates a dependent class of thinking, which can infect the entire populace. Too many can become "takers" instead of "producers." This is essentially socialism at its worst. "Why should I work if others do not? Why shouldn't the government take care of me?" And politicians simply outdo each other in promises in order to garner votes.

Chapter 6

The Best Tax for Maximum Freedom

We can thank election-driven politicians for the monstrous tax code that has put campaign contributors before ordinary taxpayers.

Author Michael Graetz makes that point well in his book, *100 Million Unnecessary Returns: A Simple, Fair, and Competitive Tax Plan for the United States*. Yet Graetz isn't a fan of "fair tax" or "flat tax" proposals. He proposes, rather, to shift the income tax largely to a value added tax and thereby eliminate the filing of income tax returns for families with incomes under $100,000. Households earning higher amounts would pay a bracketed, marginal income tax rate, ranging from 14 percent up to 31 percent for those earning incomes of $600,000 or more. He argues that his plan would simplify the tax system and take more than 150 million individuals off the IRS tax rolls.

I flatly disagree with Graetz for two important reasons:

First, and most important, the VAT would impose a tax on trade and business! Yet trade and business are the lifeblood of any economy and especially important to a free market economy.

Secondly, I sincerely believe that *all* people should pay a tax whether it's on their income or wealth.

The underlying motive for a flat tax on wealth is to provide the fairest possible tax base that applies to everyone, no exceptions. It's the best possible straight tax on wealth, unredeemable by any special escape clauses.

With a flat tax on wealth, Congress could stop fiddling with tax code adjustments and attend to the other social elements that so confound us today.

WHY THE FLAT TAX ON WEALTH IS THE BEST TAX

A flat tax on wealth is superior in its neutrality, as well as fair and transparent. It is:

"Income" neutral

"Wealth" neutral

"Conservative/Liberal" neutral

"Political Party" neutral

"Married/Single" neutral

"Lifestyle" neutral

"Own/Rent" neutral

"Young/Old" neutral

"Urban/Rural" neutral

"Employed/Unemployed/Retired" neutral

"Rich-poor/Late-Soon" neutral

"Inherited/Earned" neutral

"Sweet Charity" neutral

Let's take a more in-depth look at the neutrality of a flat tax on wealth.

"INCOME" NEUTRAL

There are many flaws in the present personal income tax system, the most glaring of which is that it simply allows the wealthiest of us to escape reasonable taxation while the working middle class continue to bear a considerable part of the burden.

In our zeal to hit the rich, we impose extreme taxation on their income. They avoid further tax by purchasing things they want, such as mansions, yachts, and airplanes, which do not produce income. Once they own what they want, their need for income as a proportion of their wealth is greatly diminished.

"WEALTH" NEUTRAL

Destroying a wealthy man's estate by taking nearly half of it with the current "death tax" is flat wrong. What have we accomplished through that sadistic act of revenge? And why shouldn't the poor pay at the same rate as the wealthy? They benefit proportionately far more from government largesse than any other income (or wealth) group. Is one or two percent beyond their means? Obviously not. And if the tax is beyond their means, it simply reflects the fact that we, as individuals, as a group, or as a nation, should not buy what we cannot afford. If we cannot pay for it, we cannot have it, either as an individual or as a nation. ONLY when we learn this lesson will we ever bring to heel the big spenders that have nearly wrecked our country, economically, in the past dozen or so years.

"CONSERVATIVE/LIBERAL" NEUTRAL

The rabid right blame the loony left for our current financial difficulties, ignoring the "conservatives" who took us into the two longest and most expensive wars in our nation's history, creating more enemies than we have ever had in the past. The loony left has compounded our debt problem severalfold and now promises to solve that debt by spending even more money that we do not have. This is madness compounded.

"POLITICAL PARTY" NEUTRAL

The Democrats blame the Republicans for creating the mess we are in. True enough. The Republicans blame the Democrats for making the mess worse. Equally true. This standoff has created an opening for the Libertarians, and the Tea Partiers, both that want not better government, but less government, whether good or bad. To heck with what's best for the country or its people. The government is seen as "the enemy," not the possible solution.

"MARRIED/SINGLE" NEUTRAL

In my admittedly very biased view, there is tremendous merit in children having two parents, one male and one female, but our tax system should not be the basis for pushing people into marriage. Although two can live nearly cheaply as one, tax code or economics is the wrong basis for forcing such a choice. Let each of us, as individuals, pay our tax on our own wealth. Marriage and divorce are sufficiently fraught without the added burden of federal income tax considerations.

"LIFESTYLE" NEUTRAL

Some have argued that the federal "death tax" should take 100 percent of a man's estate on his demise. That would force everyone to start life on an equal footing. Moreover, since the wise man would be unable to leave anything to his heirs, he would likely spend it all or give it to favored friends or relatives before that moment, thus stimulating the economy. While this is the most intriguing argument I have yet heard for such a bizarre tax, in my opinion it runs contrary to my view that a maximization of freedom is the greatest gift one has in our country. I think a man should be able—and free—to spend or to save for his heirs, as it pleases him, without coercion by such an insane tax.

"OWN/RENT" NEUTRAL

Here again I believe that the present tax system that allows an individual to deduct the interest on his mortgage payment is unjustified. Whether he chooses to rent or own, he should be free to make his own choice. The government will lose no money either way. There is no overriding national benefit to people living in individual homes as opposed to living in a condo or an apartment. While I myself much prefer to live in a single-family home, this should be an individual's choice, based entirely on what he wants and what he can afford.

"YOUNG/OLD" NEUTRAL

While it may seem an imperative kindness to the elderly to give them preferential tax treatment when they are no longer able to work and to provide for themselves, I believe it would foster a more responsible lifestyle if they were to save and invest during their working lives. Clearly, this will be a major change and one that must be introduced slowly. But in Singapore today, it is my understanding that everyone pays into a retirement fund, which is independently managed, out of the hands and control of the government. Those funds are sometimes loaned to the government to build infrastructure and earn interest paid by the government on which the retirees can live. As I am not familiar with the details of this plan nor how well it has worked out, I am in no position to argue its merits or otherwise.

"URBAN/RURAL" NEUTRAL

It might seem that a tax on wealth would unduly penalize rural families that have farmed as a way of life for generations and could lose their farm altogether if a 2 percent flat tax on wealth were imposed. Farming is an inherently risky business and might generate high income in some years, yet create the necessity for borrowing in others. Yet most farm production today is corporate or co-op farming. Furthermore, farm subsidies are extremely costly to us as a nation. Many smaller farms are share cropped so that valuing any given farm becomes difficult. Yet it should be done. How can one justify one man's working at minimum wage to pay taxes unpaid by the farmer's great-great granddaughter? It is simply irresponsible. Do not many farmers have a day job? What about farms that are put into a soil bank? How are they valued?

While this is one of the more complex issues presented by my proposal, we must wrestle with it.

SWEET CHARITY

We have become so conditioned to the ideas of "giving back," alms for the poor, and, in general, using the tax code to support our individual concepts of "social engineering" that we often lose sight of the harm done, unwittingly, by these noble aims. In the present case, I believe that in one sense, "charitable" donations destroy the concept of charity itself. I am fully aware of the great institutions created by wealthy individuals—the Carnegie libraries, superb museums, hospitals, etc. My proposal does not prevent such gifts and, in fact, when such gifts are made, it proves beyond doubt that such gifts are truly charitable and not motivated by tax avoidance.

There is no question that we should espouse a generous belief in charity and give of ourselves to worthy causes. I've already mentioned that, all too often, such causes benefit some charitable creation which employs a close friend, a relative, colleague or business associate of the beneficiary.

Another aspect could be looked at this way. The Harvard alum, in good conscience, makes a tax-deductible charitable gift to his alma mater and legally avoids taxes he must otherwise pay. But someone else has to pay those taxes, one way or another. Should the guy who works for minimum wage as a day laborer support the college of his wealthy counterpart who makes a charitable donation? Why should an atheist have to pay the otherwise unpaid taxes of the devout local priest? Or a Lutheran preacher pick up the tab for a devout believer in Islam?

How can one reasonably argue for charitable deductions? If you suggest that they promote the greater benefits of worthwhile causes, are you also suggesting that without such tax benefits, those contributions would not be made? If yes, then you have instantly destroyed the very meaning of charity!

I am all for charity. I am totally opposed to tax deductions for charitable causes. It is contrary to the true concept of "charity."

"LATE-SOON" NEUTRAL

One of the hallmarks of social engineering is the concept of taking a large bite out of the estate of the wealthy at the time of death. For me, this is preposterous. Fortunately, the FTOW does not wait until death; it takes one or two percent of his wealth away from every individual every year. But it takes relatively little. And many people today pay more in the actual dollar amount of their present tax on income than they would at this rate on their wealth.

It is flat wrong to take a large piece of life savings from any individual. Some people spend every penny of their gain during their lifetime. Others will scrimp, save and invest, providing capital for the economy to grow. Yes, the spender supports jobs. But so does the saver, as a capitalist. How can one indict one and praise the other? My flat tax on wealth is neutral. It permits people the freedom to live as they wish.

"RICH-POOR" NEUTRAL

Here is the easy one. In our desire to take from the richest among us to help the poor, we fail to understand the very nature of wealth. FTOW, as an absolutely neutral tax, would inherently and fairly tax enormous, protected family estates of the wealthy. There would be no escaping the one or two percent tax on wealth provided by this concept. Of course the progressive left will howl with pain. And so will the families of the great estates.

But how can anyone argue that any man, any household, escape paying their fair share of federal taxes? And what fairer share can there possibly be than a tax in which all pay at the same flat rate? In 2011, 46 percent of the people paid no federal income taxes, although they are still subject to sales and payroll taxes. About three-fourths of those non-payers benefitted from tax provisions aimed at low-income working families (a family of four, with an income of $26,400, for example) and senior citizens, according to the nonpartisan Tax Policy Center.

The poor benefit from the state in many ways in which the rich never will—food stamps, medical insurance, housing subsidies—out of all proportion to their contribution. Nor do I expect them to have to pay anywhere near the actual cost of such benefits—they'll pay nothing, in fact, if they have no assets. But I insist they must pay the same flat percentage of their wealth as do the rich. There is simply no other fair way!

"INHERITED-EARNED" NEUTRAL

What does it matter, strictly from a tax perspective, how a man earns his wealth or spends it? I should be able to choose to spend every penny of my income, whether earned (I worked to gain that income) or un-earned (presumably from interest on savings, dividends, capital gains on investments). With FTOW, if I spend it all, then I would have no estate to be taxed, and I would pay nothing. If scrimped, saved and wisely invested much of that income, I would pay only a small percentage of my growing wealth each year.

In contrast, under the present tax system, I would owe a small fortune in taxes. Why on earth do some so desperately insist that a man surrender much of his life savings to the federal government to accomplish this gross distortion of social engineering simply because he chose to save for his family's benefit rather than spend it? Isn't it better to give that individual the freedom to choose what he wants to do with his income?

Many of those of great wealth have used that wealth to create great institutions include Oral Roberts, John Nicholas Brown (a benefactor of Brown University, one of the finest private colleges in the United States), and Andrew Carnegie, who built more than 2,500 libraries in several countries including over 1,600 in the United States. Nearly half of the country's libraries that exist today were built with construction grants paid by Carnegie. [16] It is very difficult to do this by group enrollment and politically more so for a viable Governmental institution because of the accusations of favoritism and corruption that seem sure to arise.

Chapter 7

Interrelated Tax Matters

I believe it would be beneficial to society to look closely at those who depend on government largesse to survive. In some instances, government support is justified, such as when one is too physically or mentally disabled to work or eligible for Social Security. But if taxes were structured differently, I wonder how many would be willing to work part-time. Perhaps there are millions, I imagine, who are elderly, but don't want to risk a cut in their Social Security check, or have a disability—such as a bum knee—that would allow them to work at least part-time. At the moment, any earnings can and will be used against you.

A hard look, too, is needed at those programs that reward more children with more assistance. There has to be a way to provide a safety net, without incentivizing poor choices.

LIMITS TO TAXATION

As the U.S. population ages, how can the elderly support themselves? It is going to become essential that Social Security as we know it must be drastically changed. The only possible way to do this in my opinion is to raise the retirement age. I assume that when it was created in around 1933, retirement at 65 might have seemed reasonable with an average life expectancy of about 70. Life expectancy has increased around 15 years in the interim. Given that, we need to lengthen our expectation of working years and drastically push back the eligibility age for Social Security. Clearly this will seem to be outrageous to most Americans.

Another question is pushing forward the age when youth becomes more productive. I favor some kind of compulsory national service, perhaps two years, to provide our youth with an opportunity to contribute, such as joining the Peace Corps or engaging in useful domestic endeavors. This would give them an opportunity to develop into young men and women at a critical age. Many other countries require this.

As I said early on in this treatise, this is not about how, when and where to spend our tax dollars. It is about where, when and how to collect those taxes. But in the end ...

Peter Butterfield

IF YOU CAN'T PAY FOR IT, YOU CAN'T HAVE IT!

FOOTNOTES

[1] Nina Olson, "We Still Need a Simpler Tax Code," online.wsj.com, April 10, 2009.
[2] "Can Income Tax Hikes Close the Deficit?" The Tax Foundation Fiscal Fact Series, Paper No. 217, TaxFoundation.org, 2010.
[3] Federal Income Tax Code, 2008.
[4] Russell Berman, "Boehner: GOP House majority means 'no mandate' for tax hikes," The hill.com, November 7, 2012.
[5] Angie Drobnic Holan, "President Obama signs off on continuing tax cuts for high earners," politicfact.com, December 10, 2010.
[6] Bipartisan National Commission on Fiscal Responsibility and Reform.
[7] Email in circulation discussing European tax rates, Europa, as well as press releases of taxation trends in the European Union, including the EU27 tax ratio.
[8] Froma Harrop, "Republicans overboard on yachtsman Kerry, *Traverse City Record Eagle*, August 11, 2010.
[9] Walter E. Williams, "The rich don't pay enough?" creators.com, August 28, 2012.
[10] Nina Olson, *ibid*.
[11] An interview with Edward Wolff, "The Wealth Divide: The Growing Gap in the United States Between the Rich and the Rest," www.multinationalmnitor.org, May 2003, Volume 24, Number 5.
[12] http://www.irs.gov/taxstats/indtaxstats article/0,,id=96679,00.html.
[13] *Flow of Funds Accounts of the United States,* Federal Reserve

[14] http://www.ontheissues.org/celeb/Steve_Forbes_Tax_Reform.htm.
[15] [4] John D. McKinnon, "Some Surprises in Income Tax-Free Households," *Wall Street Journal*, September 18, 2012.
[16] Carnegie libraries by state," American Volksporting Association, 1996, October 10, 2003.

Acknowledgements

I wish to acknowledge those who have helped me make this book possible, including, but not limited to …

The doctors and other medical practitioners who have kept me alive long enough and sane enough, even though I have a number of serious diseases. In particular, I'd like to thank doctors Joel A. Greenberg, Alan J. Meadows, Ethan S. VanTil, Benjamin L. Watson, Branden S. Hunter, Gregory D. Borak, E. Stephen Yeager, David M. Cheng, Michael D. Funderburk, O. George Negrea, nurses and physician assistants Kate Crittenden, R.N., Stacy Jones, M.P.T., Fran MacCrarey, R.N., and a host of others at St. Joseph's and Candler Hospital in Savannah, GA, and Munson Medical Center in Traverse City, Michigan, together with the first responders in Glen Arbor, Michigan.

Thanks also go to headmaster Harrry Hoey of Cranbrook School and the writing teachers there; Professor Israel Kapstein at Brown; science teachers like Mr. Schultz of Cranbrook and Robert M. Beyer of Brown University, who tolerated my incompetence with patience until I began to perform to their standards, which could never have happened with lesser of their ilk.

I must thank old friends from long ago, including my college roommates, high school chums, people without whom I would never have succeeded in the way I have, including: John Eden, who encouraged me to keep trying, even though I have never been an athlete; Eugene Meckley and Howard Miller, who kept insisting that I am smart no matter the documentation I submit that proves otherwise; and Tad and Molly Morris, who continued to amaze me with their genuine acumen.

Thanks also go to more recent friends, in particular, Andy Vaught, who took time to assist with punctuation, spelling and grammar; and C.F. Yang and his colleagues and family from whom I have learned so much about China and its millennial wisdom. I also want to mention my even newer friends, including Fred Langley; neighbors such as Art and Sheila Wagner; and their successors, Gary and Karen McGuffin, who display not only their legendary smarts but a kindness, tolerance, and neighborliness to a degree I have rarely found in others.

A nod also to investors with wisdom and special insight, including Ken Brennan, Roy Smith, Rodger Ibach, Fred Langley (again!) and the other Omeleteers.

I don't know many in the world of politics, but the staff members in the office of U.S. Rep. Jack Kingston have given me help of great value, in particular, Bruce Bazemore, the late Myrlene Free, and Trish DePriest.

I continue to hope for a better understanding of the views of the Skidaway Island Republican Club and its board of directors that oppose important elements of the FTOW.

Finally, I accept with gratitude, the editorial assistance of Heather Shaw, who tried hard, early on, to help me with my writing skills, despite my continually ignoring her wisdom, and now her colleague, Anne Stanton, who re-edited this entire version of FTOW, making it far better organized and greatly improving the referencing of sources so important to a document of this kind. I also want to thank Stephen Lewis for his advice. In particular, I learned the phrase "social engineering" from him and honor his understanding of that particular expression. He is a true teacher, and I am indeed grateful. And, in closing, I am grateful for my family, who have had to tolerate all my failings, illnesses, inconsistencies and bad humor for so many years. It is beyond my ability to put that gratitude into words.

www.ingramcontent.com/pod-product-compliance
Lightning Source LLC
Chambersburg PA
CBHW020708180526
45163CB00008B/2991